Building Character For The Last Generation
2

"Receive the Holy Spirit"

Original Edition

Alonzo T. Jones

Copyright ©2023
LS COMPANY
ISBN: 979-8-8690-3267-6

Content

Preface 5

Chapter 1—We Are Comforted 7

Chapter 2—Three Editorials On The Holy Spirit 10

Chapter 3—The Completeness Of The Spirit 14

Chapter 4—The Spirit Of Wisdon And Holiness 17

Chapter 5—The Spirit Directs And Brings Joy 20

Chapter 6—The Fruit Of The Spirit Is . . . Peace 24

Chapter 7—Filled In The Time Of The Latter Rain 27

Chapter 8—We Are His Witnesses 31

Chapter 9—Full Of The Holy Spirit And Wisdom 35

Chapter 10—Did You Receive The Holy Spirit? 40

Chapter 11—The Holy Spirit Has Made You Overseers 44

Chapter 12—The Holy Spirit Received By Faith 47

Chapter 13—Unless The Holy Spirit Is Received 50

Chapter 14—To Bring The New Creation To Perfection 54

Chapter 15—Bestowed And Imparted 57

Chapter 16—Keeping The Commandments 61

Chapter 17—Going On To Perfection 63

Chapter 18—Desire Spiritual Gifts 66

Chapter 19—Do Not Grieve The Spirit 68

Chapter 20—Sealing Us For Redemption 70

Chapter 21—Perfecting Us For Redemption 73

Chapter 22—The Mystery Of God 76

Chapter 23—Imputing And Imparting 81

Chapter 24—Baptized By The Spirit 85

Chapter 25—The Unity Of The Spirit 88

Chapter 26—The Spirit Teaches Us 91

Preface

In the following articles by A. T. Jones, references to God have been capitalized; "thee's and thou's" have been updated to reflect more common usage as well as other minor corrections made for the sake of readability.

Elder Jones frequently quoted from the Spirit of Prophecy and where possible these quotes are referenced in a footnote.

Only one or two of these articles were titled - most appeared under the weekly heading of "Editorial Note" or just simple, "Editorial." Subtitles have been drawn from the context of each article and added for the ease of referencing each article - otherwise most would have the same name.

Chapter 1—We Are Comforted

"Christ impressed upon His disciples that they were to ask God in prayer for the gift of the Holy Spirit; and then, placing themselves in an attitude to receive, they would receive all the gifts comprehended in the gift of the Spirit."

Jesus says, "Without me you can do nothing."

But He is gone away; He is not here as He was when He said this.

That is all right, however; for it was expedient for us that He should thus go away.

Nevertheless He says: Be not troubled: "I will not leave you comfortless: I will come to you."

We are not left comfortless, because He comes to us by the Comforter. And "the Comforter, which is the Holy Spirit," shall "abide with you forever."

The Holy Spirit brings the presence of Christ to the believer, to abide with him forever. "His Spirit in the inner man; that Christ may dwell in your hearts, . . . that you may be filled with all the fulness of God."

The Holy Spirit comes to abide with us forever. The Holy Spirit brings the presence of Christ to abide with us forever. Therefore says Jesus, "I am with you always, even to the end of the age." "I will never leave you, nor forsake you."

Jesus said, "Without me you can do nothing." It is the Holy Spirit only that brings Christ to us. Therefore it is as plain as A-B-C, and as true as the word of God, that without the Holy Spirit we can do nothing.

Professing religion, joining the church, "working in the cause," are all "nothing" without the gift, baptism, and the abiding forever of the Holy Spirit. "Ask, and it will be given to you." "Receive the Holy Spirit."

"The Lord Jesus wants all to stand in their appointed place. He makes use of one believer's influence, another's wealth, and another's attainments. On all is inscribed, Holiness to the Lord. All is sanctified and set apart for a holy purpose. All are to co-operate with God. Mind, heart, soul, and strength belong to God. We are His by creation and by redemption. "You are not your own? For you were bought at a price; therefore glorify God in your body and in your spirit, which are God's."

When Cyrus W. Field, the maker of the Atlantic cable, left home at the age of fifteen to make his way in the world, his father said to him: "Cyrus, I feel sure you will succeed; for your playmates could never get you off to play, until all the work for which you were responsible was done." That is sufficient surety that any boy will succeed. It is simply faithfulness. And faithfulness itself is success.

"He who has not sufficient faith in Christ to believe that He can keep him from sinning, has not that faith that will give him an entrance into the heaven of God." —*Manuscript 161, 1897; also in Selected Messages, book 3, p. 360.*

The Advent Review and Sabbath Herald, February 22, 1898.

Extra:

"We may have had a measure of the Spirit of God, but by prayer and faith we are continually to seek more of the Spirit. It will never do to cease our efforts. If we do not progress, if we do not place ourselves in an attitude to receive both the former and the latter rain, we shall lose our souls, and the responsibility will lie at our own door." —*Review and Herald: March 2, 1897.*

Chapter 2—Three Editorials On The Holy Spirit

Editorial 1: "The Fruit of the Spirit"

"The fruit of the Spirit is love, joy, peace, long-suffering, gentleness, goodness, faith, meekness, temperance."

In order that there may be fruit, there must be a root. It is impossible to have fruit without first having a root.

In order, therefore, to have the fruit of the Spirit to appear in the life, the Holy Spirit Himself must be the root of the life. In order that the fruit of the Spirit may appear on the tree, the Holy Spirit Himself must be the life of the tree.

It is impossible to have genuine love, or joy, or peace, or long-suffering, or gentleness, or goodness, or faith, or meekness, or temperance, to appear in the life, without having the Holy Spirit to be the root, the spring, of the life—yes, even the very life itself.

It is not genuine love that loves only them that love you, but that which loves all, even enemies. It is not genuine goodness that does good only to them that do good to you, but that which does good to all, even the unthankful and the evil. (Luke 6:32-35).

Genuine love, or joy, or peace, or long-suffering, or gentleness, or goodness, or faith, or meekness, or temperance, comes not from ourselves, it comes not from this world; it comes only from God, it is the fruit only of the Spirit of God.

All may have the fruit of the Spirit, because all may have the Spirit. "Ask, and it will be given to you." "Receive the Holy Spirit."

The Advent Review and Sabbath Herald, March 22, 1898.

Editorial 2: "Righteousness, Peace, and Joy"

"The kingdom of God is not meat and drink; but righteousness, and peace, and joy in the Holy Spirit."

The kingdom being the kingdom of God, the righteousness is only the righteousness of God, the peace is only the peace of God, and the joy is only the joy of God—joy in the Holy Spirit; it is found only in the Holy Spirit.

And "verily, verily, I say to you, Except a man be born again, he cannot see the kingdom of God."

Except a man be born again, he cannot see righteousness, he cannot see peace, he cannot see joy in the Holy Spirit.

To be born again is to be born from above. It is to be born into the things of God. It is to be born of water and the Spirit.

The things of the kingdom of God—righteousness, and peace, and joy—can be known only through the Spirit of God; for "the things of God knows no man, but the Spirit of God."

And "the kingdom of God is within you." Is righteousness and peace and joy in the Holy Spirit, within you? If not, why not?

Do you profess to be a Christian,—a citizen of the kingdom of God,—and have not the essential elements—indeed, the kingdom itself—within you?

If this be so, it can be only because you are not born of the Spirit. And "if any man have not the Spirit of Christ, he is none of His."

O, the Heavenly Father is more willing to give you the Holy Spirit than you are to give good gifts to your own children! "Ask, and it will be given to you." "Receive the Holy Spirit."

The Advent Review and Sabbath Herald, April 5, 1898.

Editorial 3: "The Pledge of Our Inheritance"

The "Holy Spirit of promise" "is the earnest of our inheritance until the redemption of the purchased possession."

An "earnest" is "a part paid beforehand on a contract, as security for the whole."

God in Christ has contracted to give us an eternal inheritance in "a better country" than this, "that is, an heavenly," having for its capital a glorious city, "whose builder and maker is God."

This inheritance is all bought and all paid for, for us. But the time has not yet fully come for the full redemption of the purchased possession.

But He who has contracted to give it to us when it shall have been fully redeemed, pays us a part beforehand, gives us an earnest, as security for the whole eternal possession.

The earnest, that part paid beforehand on the contract, is the Holy Spirit. That security for the eternal possession is the eternal Spirit.

If you have that Spirit, and as long as you have Him, you are sure of that eternal inheritance. If you have not that Spirit, you have no surety at all of the inheritance.

But the inheritance is a free gift to all; and so is the earnest, the surety, for it, a free gift to all. And that security is "that Holy Spirit of promise."

"Ask, and it will be given to you." "Receive the Holy Spirit."

The Advent Review and Sabbath Herald, May 3, 1898

Chapter 3—The Completeness Of The Spirit

God chose us in Christ "before the foundation of the world, that we should be holy and without blame before Him in love" (Eph. 1:4).

But "all we like sheep have gone astray." "They are all gone out of the way, they are together become unprofitable; there is none that does good, no, not one."

But when we were thus enemies and alienated in our minds by wicked works, when we had altogether missed that for which God chose us, He reconciled us in the body of His flesh through death, to present us holy and blameless and above reproach in His sight" (Col. 1:21, 22).

It is His, not ours, to present us thus. It cost "all the fulness of God" to do this; and only He who could pay that price could have the power, and obtain the right, to do it. And for any one but Him to undertake to "present you holy and blameless and above reproach in His sight," is to attempt the impossible.

No, no! none but He can do it. But bless the Lord, He has the power, and has purchased the right by paying the fulness of the price. The Lord has laid "help upon one that is mighty;" and He "is able to keep you from falling, and to present you faultless before the presence of His glory with exceeding joy."

He can do it.

He will do it for you, if only you will let Him.

Let him.

The number seven is used in the Bible to represent fulness, completeness.

The expression, "the seven spirits of God," therefore, that is used several times in the Bible, signifies the fulness, the completeness, of the Spirit of God.

In other words, it represents the full and complete manifestation of the Holy Spirit in all His characteristics,—in all phases of the diversities of His operations.

What, then, are these seven characteristics of the Spirit of God? If we can know how the Spirit was manifested in Christ, we shall know what are these characteristics; for He was filled with all the fulness of God.

Can we know this of Christ?—Read this: "And the Spirit of the Lord shall rest upon Him, the spirit of wisdom and understanding, the spirit of counsel and might, the spirit of knowledge and of the fear of the Lord." (Isa. 11:2).

There are just seven: count them:—

1. The Spirit of the Lord; that is, the spirit of mercy, and grace, and long-suffering, and abundance of goodness and truth, and forgiving iniquity and transgression and sin; for that is the Lord. (Ex. 34:5-7).

2. The spirit of "wisdom."

3. The spirit of "understanding."

4. The spirit of "counsel."

5. The spirit of "might."

6. The spirit of "knowledge."

7. The spirit of "the fear of the Lord."

The gift of the Holy Spirit, therefore, is the bestowal of the disposition and character of the Lord; it is the bestowal of wisdom, of understanding, or counsel, of might, of knowledge, and of the fear of the Lord, upon all who receive the gift of the Holy Spirit. And as with Jesus, it will make the receiver "of quick understanding in the fear of the Lord."

In the manifestation of the fulness of the Spirit in the church, He divides to every man severally as He will; for "to one is given by the Spirit the word of wisdom; to another the word of knowledge by the same Spirit," etc. (1 Cor. 12:8).

"Ask, and it will be given to you." "Receive the Holy Spirit."

The Advent Review and Sabbath Herald, May 17, 1898.

Chapter 4—The Spirit Of Wisdon And Holiness

Editorial: "The Spirit of Wisdom"

The Lord desires that he "may give unto you the Spirit of wisdom and revelation in the knowledge of Him."

The Spirit of wisdom is the Spirit of Christ; for He "is made unto us wisdom."

The Spirit of wisdom is the Spirit of God; for it is one of the characteristics of the manifestation of "the seven Spirits of God."

The Spirit of wisdom is the very Spirit which Christ had; for the Spirit of wisdom rested—remained, abode—upon Him. The Spirit descended "from heaven like a dove, and it abode upon Him."

The Spirit of revelation in the knowledge of Him is clearly the Spirit by whom came the revelation of the things of God; and that is plainly the Spirit of God,— the Eternal Spirit,—by whom "God has revealed" to us the deep things of God, which "eye has not seen, nor ear heard, neither have entered into the heart of man."

The Spirit of revelation is the Spirit by whom the word of God, the Scriptures, came "in old time." For "the prophecy came not in old time by the will of man: but holy men of God spake as they were moved by the Holy Spirit."

The Lord's expressed desire, therefore, is, that He "may give to you," and that you may have, the Spirit of God,—the very Spirit that Jesus had, and the very Spirit by whom the Scriptures were given. O, He desires that you may have—yes, that you may be filled with—the Holy Spirit!

"Ask, and it will be given to you." "Receive the Holy Spirit."

The Advent Review and Sabbath Herald, May 24, 1898.

Editorial: "The Spirit of Holiness"

The Lord is coming.

And without holiness, no man can see Him in peace.

Have you holiness?

How can anybody have holiness without "the Spirit of holiness"?

And how can anybody have the Spirit of holiness without the Holy Spirit?

Have you the Holy Spirit?

"Do you think that the Scripture says in vain, The Spirit that dwells in us lusts to envy?"

Then surely, with such a spirit as that, no man can see the Lord in peace.

But He says, "A new Spirit will I put within you," and "He shall . . . abide with you forever."

He does not want the spirit that lusts to envy to abide with you forever. Do you?

He wants His own Spirit—the Holy Spirit—to abide with you forever. Do you?

Thus, having the Spirit of holiness abiding with you forever, you will have holiness.

And having holiness, you can see the Lord in peace when He comes. And He is coming soon. "Get ready, get ready, get ready."

"Ask, and it will be given to you." "Receive the Holy Spirit."

The Advent Review and Sabbath Herald, June 7, 1898.

Chapter 5—The Spirit Directs And Brings Joy

Editorial: "Directed By the Spirit"

Of the angels it is written, "Are they not all ministering spirits, sent forth to minister for them who shall be heirs of salvation?"

Yet in this ministration the angels go only as they are directed by the Spirit of God; for it is written, "Whither the Spirit was to go, they went."

Now to men is written, "As every man has received the gift, and even so minister the same one to another, as good stewards of the manifold grace of God."

Thus men who are partakers of the grace of God, which brings salvation, are engaged in the same ministration as are the angels.

And as the angels engaged in this ministration only as they are directed by the Spirit of God, then how can any human being engage in it, except as he is directed by the Spirit of God?

As the angels, to perform this ministration according to the will of God must be directed by the Spirit of God, how much more must we who are so far less in power, might, and holiness, conveyed to perform the like ministration according to will of God,—how much more must we be directed by the Spirit of God!

How all-important then it is that all who profess to be God's people shall receive, shall be baptized with, the Holy Spirit!

Without this what can we do? How all-important the message which now the Lord sends to His people, "Receive the Holy Spirit"!

"Ask, and it will be given to you." "Receive the Holy Spirit."

The Advent Review and Sabbath Herald, June 21, 1898.

Editorial: "The Spirit Makes Us Know"

"At that day you will know that I am in My Father, and you in Me, and I in you" (John 14:20).

At what day?—The day the Helper would come; the day that He Himself, by the Helper, would come.

For He said, "I will not leave you orphans; I will come to you;" and, "At that day you will know that I am in My Father, and you in Me, and I in you."

Do you know this? Do you know that He is in His Father, and you in Him, and He in you?

If you do not know it, why do you not?—There can be but one reason for any one's not knowing this; that is, he has not received the Helper, which is the Holy Spirit.

For "by this we know that we abide in Him, and He in us, because He has given us of His Spirit" (1 John 4:13).

Then when He has promised that we "will know," and has abundantly and freely supplied the means by which we shall know, that "we abide in Him, and He in us," why should any one go a single hour without that blessed knowledge?

"You will know." "By this we know." Blessed, blessed knowledge! Thank the Lord!

"Ask, and it will be given to you." "Receive the Holy Spirit."

The Advent Review and Sabbath Herald, June 28, 1898.

Editorial: "Joy in the Spirit"

"The joy of the Lord is your strength" (Neh. 8:10).

Did you know that there is real reviving strength in the joy of the Lord?

It is really so, as every one can certify from experience, who knows the joy of the Lord.

How could it be otherwise? Is there not reviving and strength in mere human joy? How much more, then, in divine joy,—in joy that is the Lord's, and that comes direct from Him to the believer!

When a person is worn, and weary, and ready to faint, and just then receives a bit of joyful news, is not all his thought of faintness at once dissipated by the joy? and is not all his weariness replaced by freshness and strength, which the joy has brought?

And when that is true in affairs altogether human, how much more must it be true in affairs divine! It is so, as every one knows who know the joy of the Lord.

But how shall we be partakers of the joy of the Lord?

The joy of the Lord in human life is the fruit of the Spirit of God. "The fruit of the Spirit is. . . joy." And we cannot have the fruit without the root.

"The kingdom of God is . . righteousness and peace and joy in the Holy Spirit" (Rom. 14:17); and "indeed, the kingdom of God is within you" (Luke 17:21).

Therefore, the joy of the Lord in human life is only by the Holy Spirit. And "the joy of the Lord is your strength."

Is the joy of the Lord your strength?

Are you worn, and weary, and ready to faint? "The joy of the Lord is your strength;" and this comes only by the Holy Spirit. Have you received the Holy Spirit?

"Ask, and it will be given to you." "Receive the Holy Spirit."

The Advent Review and Sabbath Herald, July 5, 1898.

Chapter 6—The Fruit Of The Spirit Is . . . Peace

"Peace I leave with you, My peace I give to you" (John 14:27).

Where does He leave His peace?—"With you."

Then when He leaves His peace with you, isn't it with you?

Whether you accept it or not, is another question: but where is the peace of Christ, the peace of God? He says He leaves it "with you."

When you leave a thing with a person, isn't that thing there? Whether that person ever uses it, or pays any attention to it, yet isn't it there?—You know that it is.

Very well: when the Lord says, "Peace I leave with you," then is not that peace just where He leaves it? He says that He leaves it with you; then it is with you. Whether you use it or not, it is there, it is with you.

Then since He leaves it with you; and since it is with you anyhow, not because you are so good that you deserve it, not because you have earned it, but it is with you simply because He leaves it with you, take it, and enjoy it.

Yet more than this: He says, "My peace I give to you."

When He gives it to you, doesn't it belong to you? Isn't it, then, yours?

When you give something to a person, do you not count that the thing belongs to that person? And if he doubts that it does belong to him, and treats both you and it as if it does not belong to him, then are you not disappointed and grieved?—You know you are.

Yet the Lord says, and for O so long has said, "My peace I give to you."

Then when He has given it to you, doesn't it belong to you? Assuredly it does.

Yet have you gone on all these days and years without it? And do you still go on without it? Do you doubt that it really belongs to you? Do you treat both the Lord and His gift as if the gift did not belong to you? Why will you so disappoint and grieve him?

"My peace I give to you." It belongs to you, then. Why not, then, accept it, thank Him for it, and enjoy it?

"Let the peace of God rule in your hearts." Do not try to make it rule: let it. Do not try to let it rule: simply let it.

The peace of God wants to rule in your heart and life. It will rule if you will only let it: let it.

And when you let it, then "the peace of God, which passeth all understanding, shall keep your hearts and minds through Christ Jesus" (Phil. 4:7).

It will keep both your heart and your mind: you yourself can do neither. Let the peace of God rule and keep.

It will, if only you will let it: let it.

Then, too, the Spirit of God will rule in your heart, and keep your mind; for the peace of God in the life is the fruit of the Spirit. "The fruit of the Spirit is... peace."

"Peace, peace to him who is far off and to him who is near, says the Lord, and I will heal him." "The fruit of the Spirit is. . . peace."

"Ask, and it will be given to you." "Receive the Holy Spirit."

The Advent Review and Sabbath Herald, July 12, 1898.

Chapter 7—Filled In The Time Of The Latter Rain

Editorial: "Receive the Promise of the Father"

The Book of Acts is the record of the work of the Holy Spirit in the time of "the early rain."

The first thing in the book is that Jesus "was taken up," but that it was "after He through the Holy Spirit had given commandments to the apostles whom He had chosen" (Acts 1:2).

Next, the day on which He was taken up, He "commanded them not to depart from Jerusalem, but to wait for the Promise of the Father, . . . you shall be baptized with the Holy Spirit not many days from now" (vv. 4, 5).

And next, the same day, He said, "You shall receive power when the Holy Spirit has come upon you; and you shall be witnesses to Me" (v. 8).

Now we are in "the time of the latter rain," just as truly as they were in the time of "the early rain."

Through the Holy Spirit, He has now given commandment to us to receive "the Promise of the Father" and "be baptized with the Holy Spirit," not many days from now, but just now, today, while it is called today.

It is true now and forever that "You shall receive power when the Holy Spirit has come upon you."

Have you power? If no, you know why: it is because the Holy Spirit has not come upon you.

And if the Holy Spirit has not come upon you, it is because you will not receive Him.

And without Him, you cannot be "witnesses to" Christ. "Ask, and it will be given to you." "Receive the Holy Spirit."

The Advent Review and Sabbath Herald, July 19, 1898.

Editorial: "In the Time of the Latter Rain"

The Book of Acts is the record of the work of the Holy Spirit in the line of "the early rain." And we are "in the time of the latter rain;" therefore, the Book of Acts is the record of what we may all have, only in greater abundance and power.

Then they were told to "wait for the Promise," and that they would "be baptized with the Holy Spirit not many days from now." They waited. And as they waited, they asked. And as they asked, they received. "And they were all filled with the Holy Spirit" (Acts 2:4).

In this time, just now, "in the time of the latter rain," we are told to ask for rain. And "everyone who asks receives" (Matt. 7:8).

In the time of "the early rain," on that great day of wondrous filling and of power, all the multitude were told, "The promise is to you and to your children" (Acts 2:39). "Repent, and let every one of you be baptized in the name of Jesus Christ for the remission of sins; and you shall receive the gift of the Holy Spirit" (v. 38).

In this "time of the latter rain" this "promise" is to us and to our children, to the whole multitude, as certainly as it was then to them; yes, even "to all who are afar off."

None are excluded. The promise is to all, far and near. We are in the time of the promise. We are told by the Lord Himself to "ask" in this time. And we are told by him that "everyone who asks receives." (See Zech. 10:1).

O, will you not ask? "Ask, and it will be given to you." "Receive the Holy Spirit."

The Advent Review and Sabbath Herald, July 26, 1898.

Editorial: "Filled with the Holy Spirit"

In the time of the "early rain" of the gospel year, the believers were more than once "filled with the Holy Spirit."

On Pentecost "they were all filled with the Holy Spirit" (Acts 1:4).

There was in Jerusalem much, and powerful, opposition to the gospel and to the preaching of it.

Therefore "the priests, the captain of the temple, and the Sadducees" arrested Peter and John, and "put them in custody" (Acts 4:1, 3).

The next day Peter and John were brought before the national council, and were questioned as to what they had done.

"Then Peter, filled with the Holy Spirit, said to them, "Rulers of the people and elders of Israel," etc. (v. 8).

However, the council, after inquiry and answer and consultation, let them go.

"And being let go, they went to their own companions," and prayed. "And when they had prayed, . . . they were all filled with the Holy Spirit" (vv. 23, 31).

We are in the "time of the latter rain," when we are to ask for rain. The message of God now is, therefore, "Receive the Holy Spirit;" "Be filled with the Spirit."

Have you received the Holy Spirit? Have you been filled with the Spirit? If not, you are losing everything.

But even though you have received the Holy Spirit, even though you have been filled with the Spirit, please do not think for a moment that that is the end and all. Please do not settle back contentedly folding your hands and saying, "Now I have got it, and that is all."

No; even to you the message still is, "Receive the Holy Spirit." "Be filled with the Spirit." There is more than one filling with the Spirit. Go on unto perfection.

"Ask, and it will be given to you." "Receive the Holy Spirit." "Be filled with the Spirit."

The Advent Review and Sabbath Herald, August 2, 1898.

Chapter 8—We Are His Witnesses

"You are My witnesses, says the Lord" (Isa. 43:10).

Before He left them, Jesus said to His disciples that they should be witnesses to Him "in Jerusalem, and in all Judea and Samaria, and to the end of the earth" (Acts 1:8).

And this was spoken to His disciples for all time; He intended that, in each generation, His disciples should bear witness to Him, even to the end of the earth.

His disciples of that time did this in their generation: their faith was spoken, and spoken of, "throughout the whole world;" the gospel which they preached "was preached to every creature under heaven" (Col. 1:23).

The reason of this was that they had the power to do it. Jesus said to them, "You shall receive power when the Holy Spirit has come upon you; and you shall be witnesses to Me . . . to the end of the earth."

The Holy Spirit did come upon them; they did receive power. And having power to be witnesses to the end of the earth, it was easy so to witness.

And that is true yet. Any church that has the power to witness to Christ to the end of the earth can witness to the end of the earth. It will not be difficult to do what she has the power to do.

The only reason that the church in any age has not witnesses in that age to the end of the earth, is simply because she did not have the power to do it. That is what she existed for; but she could not do it, because she did not have the power.

And she did not have the power because she would not have the Holy Spirit come upon her.

Now, in this day and age, the church must witness to Christ to the end of the earth. That is solely what she exists for. But she cannot do it without the power. Men may talk and plan and work till doomsday; but the thing can never be done without the power to do it. And the power to do it lies solely in having the Holy Spirit come upon the disciples.

And when the Holy Spirit does come upon us, making us witnesses, then He also Himself is a witness with us.

We are to witness to Jesus Christ risen from the dead, and alive now, though once dead.

This is that to which the disciples then witnessed, and to which the Holy Spirit witnessed; and this is that to which the disciples must always witness,—a risen, living Savior.

They said, "This Jesus God has raised up, of which we are all witnesses" (Acts 2:32). "And killed the Prince of life, whom God raised from the dead, of which we are witnesses" (Acts 3:15). "And we are His witnesses to these things, and so also is the Holy Spirit whom God has given to those who obey Him" (Acts 5:32).

The Holy Spirit witnesses with the believer who witnesses that Christ is risen from the dead, and is alive and at the right hand of God, to give repentance, forgiveness, and power.

It is a great and mischievous mistake to think that those disciples who were then in Jerusalem, and who saw Him with their natural eyes, were the only ones who could, or were expected to, witness to the resurrection of Christ.

We today are expected to witness to this same thing. We must witness that He is risen, and is alive today. We must witness that He is at the right hand of God, exalted to be a prince and a Savior, to give repentance and forgiveness of sins to Israel. We can do it.

We can do it because we know Him, the living Savior, with whom we live. We can do it because He lives with us. We can do it because we know that He is in us, and we in Him; and this we know by the Holy Spirit, which is given us. We can do it because He has given us the power, in giving us the Holy Spirit.

Do you know that the Holy Spirit is with you to witness unto the things which you testify of Christ? Can you cite the Holy Spirit as witness with you in what you witness unto Christ? If not, why not?

And if you cannot, then is it not because you are not, and are conscious that you are not, a true witness? And if you are not a true witness, then you are not a witness at all for Christ.

A witness is to testify to the truth, the whole truth, and nothing but the truth; he himself is to be true. "You are my witnesses, says the Lord." Are you?

Are you true? You can know. Here is the test: "He who speaks from himself seeks his own glory; but He who seeks the glory of the One who sent Him is true, and no unrighteousness is in Him" (John 7:18).

And we are witnesses of these things, and so is also the Holy Spirit. Will you be a true witness? Will you recognize the Holy Spirit as a witness also with you?

"Ask, and it will be given to you." "Receive the Holy Spirit." Recognize the Holy Spirit.

"Do not fear, little flock, for it is your Father's good pleasure to give you the kingdom" (Luke 12:32). The kingdom is not to be gained by our efforts. It is to be given to them that "do not fear." Let your mind dwell in prayerful meditation upon the infinite love of God toward you in Christ Jesus. Think of the exceeding great and precious promises, of the Holy Spirit, which dwells in you, of the holy angels that are encamped about you; think of all these blessings and "do not fear." Do not fear the want of temporal good. He who feeds the ravens, the sparrows, and the beasts, will feed you. "The Lord will provide," is a motto which you may write on every necessary want in life. Do not fear the power of Satan. Greater is He that is in you than all that are against you. The mighty God fights our battles; then why should we fear? Do not fear that the Lord will forsake you. His love is an everlasting love. He is married to you in Christ. "I will never leave you or forsake you." Having loved you, He will love you "to the end."

The Advent Review and Sabbath Herald, August 16, 1898.

Chapter 9—Full Of The Holy Spirit And Wisdom

In the time of the early rain, when they were all filled with the Holy Spirit, there was great unity among the believers. The whole "multitude of those who believed were of one heart and one soul" (Acts 4:32).

This unity stood the test of practical things, too; for "neither did anyone say that any of the things he possessed was his own, but they had all things in common" (Ibid.).

Accordingly, "nor was there anyone among them who lacked; for all who were possessors of lands or houses sold them, and brought the proceeds of the things that were sold, and laid them at the apostles' feet; and they distributed to each as anyone had need" (Acts 4:34, 35).

Presently, however, it occurred that the widows of the Grecians were neglected in the daily distribution of the funds and provisions that were common to all. And because of this, the Grecians murmured against the Hebrews.

Then the apostles "summoned the multitude of the disciples and said, "It is not desirable that we should leave the word of God and serve tables. Therefore, brethren, seek out from among you seven men of good reputation, full of the Holy Spirit and wisdom, whom we may appoint over this business; but we will give ourselves continually to prayer and to the ministry of the word" (Acts 6:2–4). This pleased the brethren all, and action was taken accordingly.

The record of this occurrence was made for us. This is true, simply because it is Scripture. But further than this, we are directed especially to study this particular part of the sixth chapter of Acts. Therefore let us study it: —

1. The apostles said, and it is written for our instruction, that it was not desirable that they should leave the word of God, and serve tables.

2. This serving of tables was the ministration, to widows and others, of the things to which they were entitled.

3. It involved the handling of money, the dealing in provisions, and the distribution of money or provisions of all sorts to the disciples. It was, therefore, very aptly designated by the apostles as "business."

Then, as this "serving tables" was the engaging in "business," when the apostles said, "It is not desirable that we should leave the word of God and serve tables," they said, It is not desirable that we should leave the word of God, and engage in business.

Inspiration says that it is not desirable that ministers of the gospel should leave the word of God and attend to business. In the time of the early rain, this was accepted and acted upon. How long shall we continue "in the time of the latter rain" before it shall be accepted and acted upon?

Bear in mind, too, that this was not a question of really quitting the ministry of the word, and engaging in business as a separate thing. It was simply a question of ministers of the gospel being occupied with the legitimate business of the church,—such strictly legitimate and sacred business as is connected with distributing provisions to widows.

Inspiration says that it is not desirable that ministers of the gospel should leave the word of God and serve business, even such as that. And the record shows that to serve business, even such as that, is to "leave the word of God."

For the apostles, the only ministers of the gospel at that time, to serve that "business" was to leave the word of God. They said so, and said that "it is not desirable" that it should be so. And when inspiration has endorsed that, and repeated to us that it "is not desirable," then why should it not be so, and how long shall it be before it shall be so, that ministers of the everlasting gospel now may leave business and serve the word of God, rather than leave the word of God and serve business, as so many now do?

When the word of God says that a thing is not desirable, no amount of "reasoning" can make it desirable. The word of God does say that it is not desirable that ministers of the gospel should leave the word of God and serve business—even the legitimate business of the church and cause of God. And no amount of "reasoning" can make such a course desirable. All such reasoning is simply setting up personal opinions and selfish preferences against the word of God - this is not Christianity: it is Christianity to cast "down arguments and every high thing that exalts itself against the knowledge of God, bringing every thought into captivity to the obedience of Christ" (2 Cor. 10:5).

In the time of the early rain, when they were all filled with the Holy Spirit, the ministers of the gospel said that "it is not desirable that we should leave the word of God, and serve business." At that time, also, the saying pleased the whole multitude. And now, in the time of the latter rain, if the ministers of the gospel would say this very same thing, the saying would again please the whole multitude.

And why should not the ministers of the gospel say it now? Indeed, why do they not all say it? Is it because they are not all filled with the Holy Spirit, as those were who did say it for our instruction? What other cause can there be? And in this time of the latter rain, when all are to be filled with the Holy Spirit as at the first, how can this thing continue against divine, true reason, unless it be that ministers of the gospel would rather leave the word of God and serve business than to seek to be so filled with the Holy Spirit that they would see and say that it is desirable to leave business and serve the word of God?

"Receive the Holy Spirit" (John 20:22). Let the ministers of the gospel receive the Holy Spirit. Let all the multitude of the believers receive the Holy Spirit. Let all, both ministers and the multitude, "be filled with the Spirit." Then the ministers will call the disciples unto them, and say: "It is not desirable that we should leave the word of God and serve tables. Therefore, brethren, seek out from among you seven men of good reputation, full of the Holy Spirit and wisdom, whom we may appoint over this business; but we will give ourselves continually to prayer and to the ministry of the word"

Then it will be again as it was before. The saying will please the whole multitude; they will choose men "full of the Holy Spirit and wisdom," whom they will set before the ministers, who will pray, and lay their hands upon them. Then, too, as before, the word of God will increase; the number of the disciples will multiply greatly, and a great company of the priests will be obedient to the faith: the office and work of the minister of the gospel will be honored as it should be, and as it is not now; and there will not be the dearth of ministers that there is now.

The Book of Acts is a record of the working of the Holy Spirit, when He had His way in the church. The sixth chapter of Acts is a part of that record, and this is what it says. With special reference to this subject, we are directed by the Spirit to "study the sixth chapter of Acts." Will you study it with the Spirit? Will you hear what the Spirit says to the churches? Will you follow the way that He leads? Will you receive the Holy Spirit? Will you be filled with the Spirit?

"Ask, and it will be given to you." "Receive the Holy Spirit." Recognize the Holy Spirit.

The Advent Review and Sabbath Herald, August 23, 1898.

Chapter 10—Did You Receive The Holy Spirit?

After the apostles had said to the multitude of the disciples that it was not reason that they should leave the word of God and attend to "business" affairs; and after the seven were chosen, among whom was Stephen, and were set over the "business," not only did the word of God greatly increase under the ministry of the apostles, but the power of God was greatly magnified in the work of the business men who were chosen.

For Stephen, "a man full of faith and the Holy Spirit," preached Christ to the council; and in resisting his words they "resisted the Holy Spirit." "But he, being full of the Holy Spirit, gazed into heaven and saw the glory of God, and Jesus standing at the right hand of God" (Acts 6:7; 7:55).

Then Philip, one of these seven, preached with great power in Samaria; and Peter and John went over and joined him: and the apostles "laid hands on them, and they received the Holy Spirit" (Acts 8:17).

Then "the angel of the Lord" sent Philip down to the road that leads from Jerusalem to Gaza; and when he arrived at that road, he saw a chariot passing, in which was a man of Ethiopia; and "the Spirit said to Philip, "Go near and overtake this chariot." Philip did so, preached to him Jesus, and baptized him; "now when they came up out of the water, the Spirit of the Lord caught Philip away" (Acts 8:29, 39).

And Saul, "still breathing threats and murder against the disciples of the Lord," near Damascus was overtaken by the Lord, and was led blind into Damascus, where Ananias was sent to him to say, "Brother Saul, the Lord Jesus, who appeared to you on the road as you came, has sent me that you may receive your sight and be filled with the Holy Spirit." "Then the churches throughout all Judea, Galilee, and Samaria had peace and were edified. And walking in the fear of the Lord and in the comfort of the Holy Spirit they were multiplied" (Acts 9:1, 17, 31).

Then the Lord had Cornelius send for Peter, who came to him and preached Christ; and while Peter was speaking, "the Holy Spirit fell upon all those who heard the word" (Acts 10:44).

The gospel spread to Antioch "unto the Grecians," which, when it came to the ears of the church in Jerusalem, "they sent out Barnabas that to go as far as Antioch." "For he was a good man, full of the Holy Spirit and of faith. And a great many people were added to the Lord" (Acts 11:22, 24).

In the church that was at Antioch there were "certain prophets and teachers;" and "as they ministered to the Lord and fasted, the Holy Spirit said, "Now separate to Me Barnabas and Saul [Paul] for the work to which I have called them." Then, having fasted and prayed, and laid hands on them, they sent them away" (Acts 13:2, 3).

In the council of the apostles and elders that was held at Jerusalem, the conclusive proof that God would have the gospel preached to the Gentiles was that He was "giving them the Holy Spirit," even as to the apostles and elders from the Jews. And when the conclusion of the council was formulated, it read: "It seemed good to the Holy Spirit, and to us" (Acts 15:28).

When Paul had gone "through Syria and Cilicia, confirming the churches," and had come to Derbe and Lystra, and "had gone throughout Phrygia and the region of Galatia," he was "forbidden by the Holy Spirit to preach the word in Asia. And after they were come to Mysia, they assayed to go into Bithynia: but the Spirit did not permit them." Then, passing by Mysia, Paul came to Troas. And now, being at the sea, as far as he could go forward by land, and forbidden by the Holy Spirit to preach the word anywhere in the region behind him, there the Spirit opened the way before him. "A vision appeared to Paul in the night: A man of Macedonia stood and pleaded with him, saying, "Come over into Macedonia, and help us" (Acts 16:1-10).

When Paul came to Ephesus, and there found certain disciples, the first question that he asked them—the first thing he said to them after the customary greeting—was, "Did you receive the Holy Spirit when you believed?" (Acts 19:2). They had not heard of the Holy Spirit, knowing only John's baptism. Paul explained that there was something beyond John's baptism,—that the object of John's baptism had come in the Lord Jesus, who had ascended again to heaven, and had sent the Holy Spirit to baptize all believers in Jesus, buried and risen from the dead. "When they heard this, they were baptized in the name of the Lord Jesus. And when Paul had laid hands on them, the Holy Spirit came upon them" (Acts 19:5, 6).

Thus in the time of the early rain, the first inquiry of disciples was, "Have you received the Holy Spirit?" and the first work of the visiting minister was to see that they had received the Holy Spirit. We are "in the time of the latter rain," which is to be more abundant than was the former. How much more abundantly, then, is it now the proper inquiry of disciples everywhere, first of all, "Did you receive the Holy Spirit when you believed?" and the first thing of all in the work of the ministry to see that they have received the Holy Spirit. These things were all written for us. Did you received the Holy Spirit when you believed?

"Ask, and it will be given to you." "Receive the Holy Spirit." "Be filled with the Spirit." Recognize the Holy Spirit.

The Advent Review and Sabbath Herald, August 30, 1898.

Chapter 11—The Holy Spirit Has Made You Overseers

As Paul was on a journey from Macedonia to Jerusalem, he paused at Miletus, and "sent to Ephesus and called for the elders of the church" (Acts 20:17).

To these elders he said words which have been preserved by inspiration for the instruction of the church, and of the elders of the church, for all time.

Among these words to the elders of the church are these: "Therefore take heed to yourselves and to all the flock, among which the Holy Spirit has made you overseers" (Acts 20:28).

Elders of the churches today, do you know that the Holy Spirit has made you overseers of the flock of God? If you did not know it before, there stands the word of God, and there it has stood all the time, telling you that it is so.

When the Holy Spirit has placed you in the responsible position of overseers of the flock of God, how are you discharging your responsibility to Him who "has made you overseers"?

Do you constantly recognize, and live in the presence of, the fact that the Holy Spirit has made you overseers? Do you constantly recognize your responsibility to the Holy Spirit? Do you constantly seek to discharge that responsibility under the guidance of the Holy Spirit, and acceptably to Him?

If not, then what are you doing in that position? Is it possible that any elder of a church will say that the Holy Spirit has not made him an overseer of the flock? If such a thing be possible, then the question recurs. What can a man be doing in a position which is under the direct supervision of the Holy Spirit, while saying that the Holy Spirit has not called him to that position? If such an attitude would not be lying to the Holy Spirit, or else entirely usurping the place of the Holy Spirit, it would certainly be perilously near it.

The church is "built together for a dwelling place of God in the Spirit." The church is under the special care of the Holy Spirit. The eldership is under the direct supervision of the Holy Spirit. And the man who occupies the position of elder stands in that relationship to the Holy Spirit, whether or not that man recognizes the fact. It is a dangerous, yes, a perilous, thing to occupy a position which is under the direct jurisdiction of the Holy Spirit, and at the same time not recognize His jurisdiction.

Surely, then, it could never be that any elder of a church would say that the Holy Spirit has not made him an overseer of the flock.

Very well, then, brethren, elders of the churches, as the word of God says that "the Holy Spirit has made you overseers," do you recognize that fact? Do you constantly live and work in the presence of that solemn and thrice-blessed fact? Do you pray in the Holy Spirit? Do you recognize the Holy Spirit in . . . oversee the flock with eyes anointed with the Holy Spirit? Do you "feed the church of God, which He has purchased with His own blood"—do you feed the church with the Bread which came down from heaven, through the power and presence of the Holy Spirit?

Elders of the churches, wherever you are, whoever you are, never forget that the word of God says that "the Holy Spirit has made you overseers" of the flock of God. Acknowledge it. Court it. Live in the presence of it. Receive that word; receive the truth expressed in that word; and receive the Holy Spirit, which has given the word in which is expressed the truth that "the Holy Spirit has made you overseers."

"Ask, and it will be given to you." "Receive the Holy Spirit." "Be filled with the Spirit."

The Advent Review and Sabbath Herald, September 6, 1898.

Chapter 12—The Holy Spirit Received By Faith

When Paul and his company had sailed away from Miletus, by Coos, and Rhodes, and Patara, and had come to Tyre, there they found disciples, and remained with them a week. And these disciples "told Paul through the Spirit not to go up to Jerusalem" (Acts 21:4).

When they had gone from Tyre, and had met the brethren at Ptolemais and stayed with them one day, they came to Cæsarea, where they tarried many days. While they were at Cæsarea, there came from Judea a prophet, who took Paul's belt, and, binding his own hands and feet, said, "Thus says the Holy Spirit, 'So shall the Jews at Jerusalem bind the man who owns this belt, and deliver him into the hands of the Gentiles.'"

After all this had come to pass, with many other vicissitudes, Paul was finally brought to Rome. At Rome he called the chief of the Jews together, and told them how it was that he had been brought thither. "So when they had appointed him a day, many came to him at his lodging, to whom he explained and solemnly testified of the kingdom of God, persuading them concerning Jesus from both the Law of Moses and the Prophets, from morning till evening. And some were persuaded by the things which were spoken, and some disbelieved. So when they did not agree among themselves, they departed after Paul had said one word: "The Holy Spirit spoke rightly through Isaiah the prophet," etc. (Acts 28:23–25).

Thus the book of Acts begins and ends with the mention of the Holy Spirit; and all the way between the beginning and the end, the Holy Spirit is recognized and received. He is constantly deferred to; He is ever and everywhere recognized as being present as witness, counselor, and guide.

That was the time of the early rain. The book of Acts is the inspired record of that time. It is the record of the working of the Holy Spirit in the time when He was recognized and allowed to reign. It was written for our instruction. And now, in "the time of the latter rain," when again the Holy Spirit is to be recognized and allowed to reign, the book of Acts is especially present truth.

The message of God today is, "Receive the Holy Spirit." But the Holy Spirit is to be received only for service; only for guidance into a deeper, more thorough, and more stable experience; only unto sanctification: never for self-gratification. And in this time the book of Acts should be carefully, diligently, and reverently studied, that we may know the way of the Spirit in His wonderful working.

Have you received the Holy Spirit since you believed? If not, why? He is freely given; you are urged by the Lord to receive Him; why do you not receive the Holy Spirit, and be filled with the Spirit?

Do you say that you do not know how? Do you know how to receive the forgiveness of sins? If you do, you know how to receive the Holy Spirit. The Lord tells you to confess your sins, and that He is faithful and just to forgive you. You confess your sins, accept His forgiveness, and then thank Him for it. You know you are forgiven, for He says so.

Do you know how to receive the righteousness of God? If so, you know how to receive the Holy Spirit. Righteousness is the free gift of God, and is received by believing God. It is received by faith. So, also, is the promise of the Spirit received by faith. The Holy Spirit is received precisely as any other gift is received from God.

He tells you, Ask for the Holy Spirit, and He shall be given you. "if we ask anything according to His will, He hears us. And if we know that He hears us, whatever we ask, we know that we have the petitions that we have asked of Him" (1 John 5:14, 15).

Ask for the Spirit: by so doing, you ask according to His will. Then, having asked, you know you have received, because He says so. Then thank Him, and continue to thank Him, that you have received the Holy Spirit. How you may feel has nothing to do with it. It is not how you feel; it is what He says.

"Ask, and it will be given to you." "Receive the Holy Spirit." "Be filled with the Spirit."

The Advent Review and Sabbath Herald, September 13, 1898.

Chapter 13—Unless The Holy Spirit Is Received

Editorial: "Unless the Holy Spirit is Received . . ."

There is a difference between "the gift of the Holy Spirit" and "the gifts of the Holy Spirit;" between the gift of the Spirit and the gifts of the Spirit.

The gift of the Holy Spirit is the gift of His Spirit bestowed by the Lord upon those who believe and are baptized in His name.

The gifts of the Holy Spirit are certain powers and operations imparted by the Holy Spirit Himself to those who have received the gift of the Holy Spirit.

Plainly enough, the gifts of the Holy Spirit can be manifested only in those who have received the gift of the Holy Spirit.

All the gifts of the Spirit—wisdom, knowledge, faith, healing, miracles, prophecy, teaching, discerning of spirits, tongues, interpretation of tongues, helps, governments—belong in the church now.

The Lord longs to see all these gifts and powers manifested in the church now. Many people, also, long to see all these gifts manifested in the church now: some, indeed, desire this more out of curiosity, or to benefit themselves, than for anything else; yet they do desire to see it.

But how can there be manifestations of the Spirit where there is not the Spirit? How can the gifts of the Spirit be imparted, where the gift of the Spirit has not been allowed to be bestowed? How can the gifts of the Holy Spirit be manifested where the gift of the Holy Spirit has not been received?

How can the church have the gifts of the Spirit, which belong in the church, until the church has first received the gift of the Spirit? And since the church is but the collection of the individuals who belong to the church, how can the church receive the gift of the Holy Spirit until the individuals who compose the church have received the gift of the Holy Spirit?

Then is it not perfectly plain that, of all things, the one essential thing—first, last, and all the time—is that each and every individual member of the church receive the Holy Spirit?

And now the Lord has sent, and is sending, to all the church throughout the whole land, the gracious essential message, "Receive the Holy Spirit." O, who can fail to respond to the gracious call? "Ask the Lord for rain in the time of the latter rain" (Zech. 10:1). Let every soul ask.

"Ask, and it will be given to you." "Receive the Holy Spirit." "Be filled with the Spirit."

The Advent Review and Sabbath Herald, September 20, 1898.

Editorial: "Gifts to Each One Individually"

The gift of the Holy Spirit is to all believers alike.

The gifts of the Holy Spirit are diverse, "to each one individually as He wills."

For in the gifts of the Holy Spirit, "for to one is given the word of wisdom through the Spirit, to another the word of knowledge through the same Spirit, to another faith by the same Spirit, to another gifts of healings by the same Spirit, to another the working of miracles, to another prophecy, to another discerning of spirits, to another different kinds of tongues, to another the interpretation of tongues. But one and the same Spirit works all these things, distributing to each one individually as He wills" (1 Cor. 12:8–11).

But how can the Spirit in His gifts distribute to each one individually, unless each one individually has first recognized and received the gift of the Spirit?

And as the Spirit cannot in His gifts divide to each one individually, unless men individually recognize and receive the gift of the Spirit, it is clear that both in the gift of the Spirit and in the gifts of the Spirit, it is altogether an individual matter.

The Holy Spirit is never poured out on companies, except as He is poured out upon individuals in the companies.

The Spirit was poured out upon the whole company, more than once, as recorded in the book of Acts; but this was only because He was poured out upon each individual in the company. Each individual was ready to receive the Spirit; and being poured in His fullness upon each individual in the company, in the nature of the case He was poured out upon the whole company.

If in a company of people there were one person who was not prepared to receive the Holy Spirit, and the Spirit were poured out upon that company, in that case the Spirit would not be poured upon that individual.

The Spirit could be poured upon the company, only by being poured upon the individuals of the company, and could extend only so far as the individuals were ready to receive Him.

Since, then, the receiving of the gift of the Holy Spirit is altogether an individual matter, and as it lies altogether between the individual and the Lord, it is plain that the gift of the Holy Spirit can be received by the individual just where the individual is, whenever the individual is ready. For on the Lord's part the gift is free. And "now is the accepted time."

"Ask, and it will be given to you." "Receive the Holy Spirit." "Be filled with the Spirit."

The Advent Review and Sabbath Herald, September 27, 1898.

Chapter 14—To Bring The New Creation To Perfection

It must never for a moment be forgotten that the great object of the gift of the Holy Spirit is the perfecting of the receiver of the gift.

Whosoever receives, or would receive, the gift of the Holy Spirit, frustrates the very purpose of the gift unless he believes in Christian perfection, and unless he expects the Holy Spirit to bring him unto perfection.

This is taught and illustrated in the very first chapter in the Bible: "In the beginning God created the heavens and the earth. The earth was without form, and void; and darkness was on the face of the deep. And the Spirit of God was hovering over the face of the waters" (Gen. 1:1, 2).

The word here translated "moved"

signifies "to brood over" and fructify. Thus when the unformed mass had been created, it was the Spirit of God which, through the spoken word of God, shaped the earth, clothed it with beauty and fruitfulness, and brought it to perfection.

Except for this gift of the Spirit to move upon the void and formless earth, and except for the further word of God and ministration of the Spirit of God, the earth would forever have remained without form and void. The object of its creation would have been utterly missed.

The only object in the creation of the earth was that it should be brought to perfection. When it had been created, the Spirit of

God was given to move upon it. And the object of this bestowal of the Spirit was that the earth, by the ministry of the Spirit, should be brought to perfection. And so this object was accomplished.

Now "we are His workmanship, created in Christ Jesus for good works, which God prepared beforehand that we should walk in them" (Eph. 2:10).

But though we are thus created unto the good works of God, yet when we have been so created, so far as the realization of these good works in action, our lives are as formless and void as was the earth when it was first created.

And unless the Spirit of God can come upon this new creation, to brood over it and fructify it with the power of God; unless the further word of God, and the ministration of the Spirit of God, shall come into the life, this new creation must forever remain as formless and void as, without it, would have remained the original creation.

Such, however, is not the object in this creation, as it was not the object of the original creation. The object in this new creation is that it shall be brought to perfection, as certainly as was the object in the original creation. And this can be done only by the gift of the Spirit of God, and the further word, and ministration of the Spirit, of God.

Therefore, every believer must constantly hold perfection in view. He must never be satisfied one moment with anything short of perfection. He must never forget that only this is the object of his having been created new in Christ Jesus. And he must never forget that this object can be accomplished only by the power and ministration of the Holy Spirit through the word of God.

"Ask, and it will be given to you." "Receive the Holy Spirit." "Be filled with the Spirit."

The Advent Review and Sabbath Herald, October 4, 1898.

Chapter 15—Bestowed And Imparted

Editorial: "The Spirit is Bestowed; the Gifts are Imparted"

The object of the gift of the Holy Spirit is the perfecting of the receivers of the gift.

The means of perfecting the receiver of the gift of the Holy Spirit is the gifts of the Holy Spirit.

The gift of the Holy Spirit is the Holy Spirit bestowed: the gifts of the Holy Spirit are gifts imparted by the Holy Spirit, that has been bestowed.

The gifts of the Spirit are, wisdom, knowledge, faith, healing, miracles, prophecy, discerning of spirits, tongues, interpretation of tongues, teaching, exhortation, helping, governing, evangelists, pastors,—"distributing to each one individually as He wills" (1 Cor. 12:11).

The purpose in the impartation of these gifts is thus declared: "He Himself gave some to be apostles, some prophets, some evangelists, and some pastors and teachers, for the EQUIPPING [PERFECTING] OF THE SAINTS" (Eph. 4:11, 12).

When the object of the gift of the Holy Spirit is the perfecting [equipping] of the receivers of the gift, and when the means of accomplishing this object is the gifts of the Holy Spirit, it is perfectly plain that both the gift and the gifts of the Holy Spirit are not an end, but only means to an end; and that end, the perfecting [equipping] of the believers.

Then what must the one great thought of all who have received, the gift of the Holy Spirit, and the impartation of the gifts of the Holy Spirit received?—Only perfection, perfection, PERFECTION,—nothing but perfection in Christ Jesus.

Therefore in this "time of the latter rain," in this day of the giving of the Holy Spirit, in this time of the receiving of the Holy Spirit, every one who will set his whole heart, yield his whole thought, to being brought to perfection in Christ Jesus, and will surrender himself to the working of the Holy Spirit, that the Spirit may accomplish God's purpose upon him, can freely receive the fulness of the Holy Spirit.

"Ask, and it will be given to you." "Receive the Holy Spirit." "Be filled with the Spirit."

The Advent Review and Sabbath Herald, October 11, 1898.

Editorial: "Agape Love, the Bond of Perfection"

The "perfecting of the saints" is the object of the gift of the Holy Spirit.

If this is not held ever in view by the believer, the purpose of the gift of the Spirit is frustrated.

The means of the "perfecting of the saints" are the gifts of the Holy Spirit; for He "gave gifts to men" "for the perfecting [equipping] of the saints."

The point which marks the perfection of the believer is love—perfect love

—the love of God; for "love. . . is the bond of perfection" (Col. 3:14).

The point which betokens love, this perfect love, the love of God, this "bond of perfection," is the keeping of the commandments of God; for "this is the love of God, that we keep His commandments." And "love is the fulfilling of the law."

Therefore, as the keeping of the commandments of God is love, and love is the bond of perfection, then the keeping of the commandments of God is the bond of perfection.

Then, as the keeping of the commandments of God is the bond of perfection, and as perfection is the object of both the gift and the gifts of the Holy Spirit, it certainly follows that the keeping of the commandments of God is the great object of the gift of the Holy Spirit.

Anybody, then, who does not have in view the keeping of the commandments of God, misses the purpose of the Lord in giving the Holy Spirit, and frustrate the object of the Holy Spirit even though He is given.

The keeping of the commandments of God is the complete manifestation, in the individual, of the perfect will of God. Anyone, then, who would think of receiving the Holy Spirit for any other purpose than to manifest the perfect will of God, could not receive the Holy Spirit. And anyone, having received the gift of the Holy Spirit, who would use the gift for any other purpose than to manifest the perfect will of God, could not retain the Holy Spirit.

Do you want the perfect will of God manifested in you? Do you want, are you willing, to keep the commandments of God? Then "receive the Holy Spirit."

"Ask, and it will be given to you." "Receive the Holy Spirit." "Be filled with the Spirit."

The Advent Review and Sabbath Herald, October 18, 1898.

Chapter 16—Keeping The Commandments

We are commanded to "desire spiritual gifts" (1 Cor. 14:1), and to "earnestly desire the best gifts" (1 Cor. 12:31).

These spiritual gifts are the gifts of the Holy Spirit, which are imparted by the Spirit to those who have received the Holy Spirit.

The sole object of these gifts is the perfecting of the of the saints,—the bringing to perfection the believers in Jesus.

Christian perfection is manifested in "love, which is the bond of perfection" (Col. 3:14). This is the love [agape] of God; "for this is the love of God, that we keep his commandments" (1 John 5:3).

So entirely is it true that love is the sole object of the gifts of the Holy Spirit, that though I had the gift of tongues in such measure that I could "speak with the tongues of men and of angels, but have not love, I have become sounding brass or a clanging cymbal" (1 Cor. 13:1). And this is the love of God, "for this is the love of God, that we keep his commandments."

So entirely is it true that love is the sole object of the gifts of the Holy Spirit, that "though I have the gift of prophecy, and understand all mysteries and all knowledge, and though I have all faith, so that I could remove mountains, but have not love, I am nothing" (v. 2). And this is the love of God; "for this is the love of God, that we keep his commandments."

So entirely is it true that the sole object of the gifts of the Spirit is love, that though I had these gifts in such measure that I were to "bestow all my goods to feed the poor, and though I give my body to be burned, but have not love, it profits me nothing" (v. 3). And this is the love of God; "for this is the love of God, that keep his commandments."

Thus is it entirely true, and the evidence is overwhelming, that the keeping of the commandments of God is the sole object of the gifts of the Holy Spirit. And thus it is demonstrated that the keeping of the commandments of God is the greatest gift that can possibly be bestowed upon men.

Do you desire to keep the commandments of God? If you do, then earnestly "desire spiritual gifts;" for without these you never can become a true keeper of the commandments of God.

Do you desire really to keep the commandments of God? If you do, then "earnestly desire the best gifts;" for only by the gifts of the Spirit can you ever be a keeper of the commandments.

"Ask, and it will be given to you." "Receive the Holy Spirit." "Be filled with the Spirit." "Earnestly desire the best gifts."

The Advent Review and Sabbath Herald, October 25, 1898.

Chapter 17—Going On To Perfection

Editorial: "Going on to Perfection"

Perfection is the only goal of any believer in Jesus.

It is the only thing set before anybody by Jesus; for he said, "Be ye therefore perfect, even as your Father which is in heaven is perfect." Matt. 5:48.

Therefore, the divine exhortation to every believer in Jesus is, "Let us go on to perfection." And the only response to this that is given for Christians, and the only response any Christian can give, is, "This will we do if God permits" (Heb. 6:1, 3).

But nobody can attain to perfection without the gifts of the Holy Spirit; for these are given "for the perfecting [equipping] of the saints," and "till we all come to the unity of the faith and of the knowledge of the Son of God, to a perfect man, to the measure of the stature of the fullness of Christ" (Eph. 4:11–13).

And nobody can have the gifts of the Holy Spirit, who has not first received the gift of the Holy Spirit.

Therefore, without the gift of the Holy Spirit, no believer in Jesus can reach the only goal that is set before him by the Lord.

Therefore, every believer in Jesus must receive the gift of the Holy Spirit. Accordingly, it is the all-important question for every minister to ask every believer, "Did you receive the Holy Spirit when you believed?" (Acts 19:2).

"Ask, and it will be given to you." "Receive the Holy Spirit." "Be filled with the Spirit." "Earnestly desire the best gifts." And "go on to perfection."

The Advent Review and Sabbath Herald, November 1, 1898.

Editorial: "Those Who Keep the Commandments of God"

So entirely is it true that the sole purpose of the gifts of the Holy Spirit is to bring to perfection the believers in Jesus, that when this shall be accomplished, these gifts will "cease" and "be done away."

Love is the bond of perfection. And as it is true that though a person were to have all the gifts, and yet had not love, it would profit him nothing, this of itself shows that perfection in the believers is the object of the gifts.

This is also shown in the fact that "love never fails. But whether there are prophecies, they will fail; whether there are tongues, they will cease; whether there is knowledge, it will vanish away." Prophecies, tongues, knowledge, and the other gifts are all given to bring us to love; but when they have brought us to love, they "fail," "cease," and "vanish away."

"For we know in part and we prophesy in part. But when that which is perfect has come, then that which is in part will be done away." Even by the gift of knowledge, we know only in part until we attain to that which is perfect. But when that which is perfect is come, we shall then know fully; we shall know even as we are known. Therefore the gift of knowledge, like all the other gifts, is given only as a means of bringing us to perfection,—to bring us to love, the bond of perfection.

"For this is the love of God, that we keep His commandments." Therefore the object of all the gifts of the Spirit is to bring the believers to the keeping of the commandments of God. And this shows that the greatest gift that can be bestowed upon men, the greatest thing that can be done for them, by the Lord, is to bring them to the keeping of the commandments of God.

This is the third angel's message; for "here are those who keep the commandments of God and the faith of Jesus" (Rev. 14:12).

"Ask, and it will be given to you." "Receive the Holy Spirit." "Be filled with the Spirit." "Desire spiritual gifts." "Earnestly desire the best gifts."

The Advent Review and Sabbath Herald, November 8, 1898.

Chapter 18—Desire Spiritual Gifts

"Desire spiritual gifts." Do you? If not, why?

Surely this is as plain an injunction as there is in the Bible. Why, then, should you not obey it?

Perhaps you will say that you have long desired to see spiritual gifts manifested in the church, and have even wondered why they were not.

But that is not what the Scripture says; it does not say, Desire spiritual gifts manifested in the church; but, "Desire spiritual gifts;" that is, Desire them manifested in yourself.

"Do you have faith? Have it to yourself before God" (Rom. 14:22). Suppose you should see all the gifts manifested in the church, and yet none of them be manifested in yourself, what good would that do? You could even see all this, and yet be lost yourself. Do you not know that thousands, yes, the whole world, will see all these gifts manifested in the church, and yet it will do them no good!

No; this is an individual matter. True, the gifts are to be manifested in the church; but this can be only by their being manifested in each individual member of the church. The gifts are divided "to every man severally."

Are you a member of the church? Do you belong to the body of Christ? Do you believe in Jesus? Then you are to desire that the gifts of the Spirit will be manifested in yourself. If this is not so with yourself, you cannot be ready to meet the Lord.

Yet to "desire spiritual gifts" is only a part of the injunction,—the subordinate part, too. The whole of it is, "Pursue love, AND desire spiritual gifts" (1 Cor. 14:1).

To desire spiritual gifts is altogether proper. Yet to do this without love's being held solely in view, would be altogether vain; because though we had all the gifts, and yet had not love, it would profit us nothing, and we would be nothing.

Then as the only true way to desire spiritual gifts is to desire them upon yourself, and as the only proper connection in which to desire them is to follow after love and desire them, it follows that you must follow after love yourself, and desire spiritual gifts manifested upon yourself in order that you may attain that thing after which you are following.

And the love after which you are to follow is the bond of perfectness, it is the love of God. And as "this is the love of God, that we keep his commandments," then it is certain that the thing after which we are to follow while we are desiring spiritual gifts, is the keeping of the commandments of God. And the keeping of the commandments of God and the faith of Jesus is the third angel's message.

There can be no true keeping of the commandments of God without love; there can be no true love without spiritual gifts; there can be no spiritual gifts without the gift of the Holy Spirit; therefore without the gift of the Holy Spirit, there can be no true third angel's message.

"Ask, and it will be given to you." "Receive the Holy Spirit." "Be filled with the Spirit." "Desire spiritual gifts."

The Advent Review and Sabbath Herald, November 15, 1898.

Chapter 19—Do Not Grieve The Spirit

For more than a year the Lord has been sending to His people the definite message, "Receive the Holy Spirit."

Thus the attention of a whole people, all round the earth, has been directed to this one definite call of God,—to this one great blessing of receiving the Holy Spirit.

Has it occurred to you to inquire as to just what this means? If not, please read this scripture, and think: "And do not grieve the Holy Spirit of God, by whom you were sealed for the day of redemption" (Eph. 4:30).

As it is by the Holy Spirit that the people of God must be sealed, and as God is especially calling upon all his people to receive the Holy Spirit, then does not this plainly show that we are now, in the time of the sealing of God's people?

If this is not plain to you, why so? Since the object of the Holy Spirit is to seal; till the day of redemption, those who receive Him; and now, for more than a year, God is calling upon all His people to receive the Holy Spirit, do you expect this call to go on forever without the object of the Holy Spirit being accomplished,— the sealing of those who receive Him? Do you expect the call to receive the Holy Spirit to go on forever, and expect the Holy Spirit to abide forever with those who do receive Him, without that Spirit's accomplishing the very object for which He is given?

If you do not expect this, then since it is only by the Holy Spirit that the sealing is done, and since God is now, and has been for more than a year, continuously calling to His people to receive the Holy Spirit, is, it not perfectly plain that we are now in the time of the sealing of God's people? And if it should be that this is not yet plain to you, then is it not because you are not looking straight in this direction? or else because you have not yet anointed your eyes with the "eye-salve, that thou mayest see"?

This will never do. No; God will not work forever, and do nothing. God will not send a message forever without accomplishing that whereunto the message is sent. And as He is now sending His message, "Receive the Holy Spirit;" and as the work of that Spirit is to seal the receivers thereof unto the day of redemption, it is certain that now is the time in which, by the Holy Spirit, God will seal His people unto the day of redemption, which, by all other signs also, is nigh at hand.

"Get ready, get ready, get ready." "Ask, and it shall be given you." "Receive the Holy Spirit." "Be filled with" the "holy Spirit of God, whereby are sealed unto the day of redemption."

The Advent Review and Sabbath Herald, November 22, 1898.

Chapter 20—Sealing Us For Redemption

"And there will be signs in the sun, in the moon, and in the stars; and on the earth distress of nations, with perplexity, the sea and the waves roaring" (Luke 21:25).

"Now when these things begin to happen, look up and lift up your heads, because your redemption draws near" (v. 28). And "when you see all these things, know that it is near—at the doors!" (Matt. 24:33).

These things began to come to pass long ago; for years we have been telling the people that this is so. But now we see all these things.

When these things began to come to pass, which was long ago, then redemption was drawing near. But now, when we see all these things, it is at the doors.

The day of redemption, therefore, is certainly now at hand. But though this is so, though there is distress of nations, with perplexity; though the nations are angry, and are ready to break forth into the time of trouble that will overwhelm all, yet the day of redemption cannot come "till the servants of our God" are sealed.

For "I saw four angels standing at the four corners of the earth, holding the four winds of the earth, that the wind should not blow on the earth, on the sea, or on any tree. Then I saw another angel ascending from the east, having the seal of the living God. And he cried with a loud voice to the four angels to whom it was granted to harm the earth and the sea, saying, "Do not harm the earth, the sea, or the trees till we have sealed the servants of our God on their foreheads" (Rev. 7:1–3).

Then as certainly as "all these things" are now seen, so certainly is the day of redemption at hand.

And as certainly as the day of redemption is at hand, so certainly is the time of the sealing of God's people near at hand, because these must be sealed before that great day.

But it is "the Holy Spirit of God, whereby you are sealed for the day of redemption."

The Lord is now, and for more than a year has been, especially calling His people to receive the Holy Spirit. And as the work of the Holy Spirit is to seal the receiver for the day of redemption, this demonstrates both that the day of redemption is at hand and that now is the time of the sealing of the servants of God, because the sealing of the servants of God must precede the day of redemption.

Thus every sign, both in the church and in the world, testifies with a loud voice that the day of redemption is at hand, and that the time of the sealing of the servants of God is also certainly at hand.

But do you want to see this clearly stated on direct authority? Here it is: "The time has come when all who work in Christ's lines will have the mark of God, in words, in spirit, in character, in their honor of Immanuel." —Testimony, Sept. 20, 1898.

God calls upon all to receive the Holy Spirit, because by the Holy Spirit "you are sealed for the day of redemption;" and "the time has come" for the servants of our God to be sealed, so that they "will have the mark of God in words, in spirit, in character, in their honor of Immanuel." Where stand you? How stand you?

"Get ready, get ready, get ready." "Ask, and it will be given to you." "Receive the Holy Spirit." "Be filled with" "the Holy Spirit of God, by whom you were sealed for the day of redemption."

The Advent Review and Sabbath Herald, November 29, 1898.

Chapter 21—Perfecting Us For Redemption

The message is advancing so rapidly that constant watching and diligent attention are required to keep pace with it. And sad it is for the one who falls behind now, whether he is a layman, or one who must bear the burden and responsibility of acting in public capacity. In order to stand, all must have a constant consecration; indeed, consecration, to be consecration, must be constant.

In 2 Chronicles 25:1, 2, we read that Amaziah reigned for twenty-nine years in Jerusalem, and that during that time "he did what was right in the sight of the Lord, but not with a loyal [perfect] heart." There are Amaziah's today, and they find it an easy matter so to conduct themselves that men adjudge their acts as "right in the sight of the Lord," but God does not accept their service. The Lord is soon coming. In that day only the "pure in heart" will see God unto salvation. Is there any one who knows these truths, and yet delays to pray, from the very depths of his soul: "Search me, O God, and know my heart; try me, and know my anxieties; and see if there is any wicked way in me, and lead me in the way everlasting" (Ps. 139:23, 24)?

"The time has come when all who work in Christ's lines will have the mark of God, in words, in spirit, in character, in their honor of Immanuel."

But God will never set His mark upon words that are not true and pure, nor upon a spirit that is not right. He will never set His seal upon a character that is not perfect, nor upon an honor of Immanuel which is not genuine.

God cannot put His seal upon anything that is in any respect short of perfection. Then as the time has come when all who work in Christ's lines will have the mark of God, this says that we are in the time when God will bring to perfection all who work in Christ's lines. Thank the Lord! What a precious promise! What a cheering thought!

But without the Holy Spirit, no one can have this mark; because it is only "the Holy Spirit of God, by whom you were sealed for the day of redemption"

Again: none can receive this mark who are in any point short of perfection; and none can have the mark, without the Holy Spirit; therefore, it is the work of the Holy Spirit now to bring to perfection all who work in Christ's lines.

The Holy Spirit is now given without measure; and the Lord is calling upon all to receive the Holy Spirit. The Holy Spirit, when given, is to impart gifts "to every man severally as he will." The object of these gifts is the perfecting of the saints. And this object will be accomplished in bringing all "in the unity of the faith, and of the knowledge of the Son of God, unto a perfect man, to the measure of the stature of the fullness of Christ."

Therefore "receive the Holy Spirit," and "covet earnestly the best gifts," that thus you may be brought to perfection, and may receive the seal of God, in words, in spirit, in character, and in your honor of Immanuel.

"In words;" because "Now we have received, not the spirit of the world, but the Spirit who is from God, that we might know the things that have been freely given to us by God. These things we also speak, not in words which man's wisdom teaches but which the Holy Spirit teaches" (1 Cor. 2:12, 13).

"In spirit;" because "if anyone does not have the Spirit of Christ, he is not His;" and if any man have the Spirit of Christ, this "is life because of righteousness" (Rom. 8:9, 10).

"In character;" because "the righteous requirement of the law might be fulfilled in us who do not walk according to the flesh but according to the Spirit" (Rom. 8:4); and "here are those who keep the commandments of God and the faith of Jesus" (Rev. 14:12).

"In their honor of Immanuel;" because they will not worship the beast or his image, neither will they receive his mark in their foreheads, or in their hands.

How good the Lord is, to give us his Holy Spirit to bring us to perfection, that we may have the mark of God in words, in actions, in character, in our honor of Immanuel; and so be sealed with the seal of the living God!

"Now may the God of peace who brought up our Lord Jesus from the dead, that great Shepherd of the sheep, through the blood of the everlasting covenant, make you COMPLETE [PERFECT] in every good work to do His will, working in you what is well pleasing in His sight, through Jesus Christ, to whom be glory forever and ever. Amen" (Heb. 13:20, 21).

"Ask, and it will be given to you." "Receive the Holy Spirit." "Be filled with" "the Holy Spirit of God, by whom you were sealed for the day of redemption." For behold "it is near, even at the doors."

The Advent Review and Sabbath Herald, December 6, 1898.

Chapter 22—The Mystery Of God

It is written that "in the days of the sounding of the seventh angel, when he is about to sound, the mystery of God would be finished" (Rev. 10:7).

The mystery of God "is Christ in you, the hope of glory" (Col. 1:26, 27).

The finishing of the mystery of God, then, is the finishing of the work of "Christ in you."

The finishing of the work of Christ in you is the bringing of you to perfection in Christ Jesus.

And the bringing of you to perfection in Christ Jesus, is by the power of the Holy Spirit, "according to the working by which He is able even to subdue all things to Himself" (Phil. 3:21).

For the Holy Spirit is given, imparting His precious gifts, expressly "for the equipping of the saints, . . . till we all come to the unity of the faith and of the knowledge of the Son of God, to a perfect man, to the measure of the stature of the fullness of Christ" (Eph. 4:12, 13).

This is promised for "the days [prophetic days—years] of the voice of the seventh [trumpet] angel, when he shall begin to sound."

The seventh angel began to sound in 1844, has been sounding ever since, and still continues to sound, and will yet continue to sound for a long time, even until all woe shall have passed from the earth.

But it is not at the end of his sounding; it is not late in the years of his sounding,—no, it is in the years when he shall begin to sound,—that the mystery of God, the work of Christ in you, shall be finished.

And as he has now been sounding fifty-four years [179 years in 2023] with the mystery of God, the work of Christ in you, not yet finished, this shows that this work has been delayed. But on the Lord's part there is never any delay: now is always the time with Him. This delay is altogether on the part of His people. The Lord's people have hesitated, and delayed to surrender themselves fully to be worked by the Holy Spirit into the complete image of the Lord Jesus. Many have delayed to have Him even begin the mystery of God, the work of Christ in them, much less finish it.

This will never do. This must not be so any more. Now is the time. These are the days. The seventh angel is sounding. The nations are angry. The wrath of God is about to fall. It is the time of the dead and the living, when they shall be judged; and when He shall give reward to the saints, and to the prophets, and to them that fear His name, both small and great. It is the time when the kingdoms of this world are to become the kingdoms of our God and of His Christ; and when He shall destroy them that corrupt the earth. (Rev. 11:15-18). O, it is the time when the mystery of God should be, yes, and will be, finished!

And the finishing of this mystery is the perfecting of the believers, even to the measure of the stature of the fullness of Christ.

The mystery of godliness is "God was manifested in the flesh" (1 Tim. 3:16). And the finishing of this mystery signifies not only the finishing of the work of God in the believer, so that the believer reflects only Christ,—all of God and none of self,—but it signifies also that this manifestation of God in the flesh will be finished, and that He will be manifest only in the Spirit: and this signifies the changing of the believers from flesh to spirit; and this signifies translation. Thank the Lord!

And now is the time. We are in the days when the mystery of God will be finished, which means that we are in the days when God will prepare His people for translation, by bringing us to perfection according to the measure of the stature of the fullness of Christ. Bless the Lord!

What a precious promise, what a blessed prospect, that is,— that you and I shall be perfect!—perfect according to God's own standard,—perfect as Christ was perfect. Yes, and perfect as He is perfect; for "we know that when He is revealed, we shall be like Him, for we shall see Him [not as He was—but] as He IS" (1 John 3:2).

"The Lord will perfect that which concerns me" (Ps. 138:8). Bless His name! It is He alone who must make any one perfect. And He will "make you perfect in every good work to do His will, working in you that which is well pleasing in His sight," "through the blood of the everlasting covenant," "through Jesus Christ; to whom be glory forever and ever. Amen."

Who can hesitate and delay any longer to yield up all to God, that He may make you perfect?

Do not think for a moment that it will take Him a long time, as it has taken you, and in vain. He does this work by creation, not by evolution. He does it, you cannot do it. He does it by His word, not you do it by your vain efforts. Read this:—

"While so many of our people have been hovering about the mystery of faith and godliness, they could have solved the matter by proclaiming, 'I know that Christ is my portion forever. His mercy, His gentleness, has made me great.'" (Testimony, Sept. 20, 1898; Ellen G. White, This Day With God, p.231)

Why not, then, solve this mystery of faith and godliness just now, when it is so easily and quickly solved? Why not let God finish His mystery in you, according to His own purpose in Christ Jesus? Why not, just now, receive His Holy Spirit in all His fulness and gracious working, that He may perfect you to the measure of the stature of the fullness of Christ? Why not?

"Ask, and it will be given to you." "Receive the Holy Spirit." "Be filled with" "the Holy Spirit of God," by whose working alone the mystery of God can be finished in you, and "by whom you were sealed for the day of redemption."

The Advent Review and Sabbath Herald, December 13, 1898.

An Extra Sidelight on Colossians 1:26, 27

Ellen White makes many statements regarding the mystery of God, which is "Christ in you, the hope of glory." In keeping with the theme of this article, three powerful comments are placed below for the readers further study. —*the editor.*

"The incarnation of Jesus Christ, the divine son of God, 'Christ in you, the hope of glory,' is the great theme of the gospel. 'In Him dwells all the fullness of the Godhead bodily. And ye are complete in Him.' " Colossians 1:27; 2:9, 10. —*Ellen G. White, Christian Experience and Teachings, p. 246.*

" 'Christ in you, the hope of glory.' A knowledge of this mystery furnishes a key to every other. It opens to the soul the treasures of the universe, the possibilities of infinite development." —*Ellen G. White, My Life Today, p. 301.*

"A large number who claim to believe the present truth, know not what constitutes the faith that was once delivered to the saints— Christ in you the hope of glory. They think they are defending the old landmarks, but they are lukewarm and indifferent." —*The Ellen G. White 1888 Materials, p. 403.*

Chapter 23—Imputing And Imparting

"The time has come when all who work in Christ's lines will have the mark of God, in words, in spirit, in character, in their honor of Immanuel."

The man who was to set the mark of God upon the people "was clothed with linen." And "the fine linen is the righteousness acts of saints" (Rev. 19:8).

This mark, then, which he sets upon the people, is the mark of the righteousness, the character, of God, "even the righteousness of God which is by [the] faith of Jesus Christ to all and upon all them that believe. For there is no difference" (Rom. 3:22).

This mark is set alone by means of the Spirit of God. "For the law of the Spirit of life in Christ Jesus has made me free from the law of sin and death. . . . that the righteous requirement of the law might be fulfilled in us who do not walk according to the flesh but according to the Spirit" (Rom. 8:2, 4).

Again: "Christ has redeemed us from the curse of the law, . . . that the blessing of Abraham might come upon the Gentiles in Christ Jesus, that we might receive the promise of the Spirit through faith" (Gal. 3:13, 14).

The blessing of Abraham is the righteousness of God. The righteousness of God comes only by faith. And when it had come to Abraham, he then received the sign of circumcision, a "seal of the righteousness of the faith which he had" (Rom. 4:11).

True circumcision is "that of the heart, in the Spirit" (Rom. 2:29). Accordingly, the gift of the Holy Spirit is the seal of the righteousness of the faith which we have. He is the seal of the righteousness of God imputed to us by faith before we are circumcised, and also the seal of the righteousness of God imparted to us through faith after we have been circumcised.

"And the Lord your God will circumcise your heart . . . to love the Lord your God with all your heart and with all your soul, that you may live" (Deut. 30:6). To love God with all the heart and with all the soul, is the bond of perfectness. It is the love of God, which is shed abroad in our hearts by the Holy Spirit, which is given to us. And "this is the love of God, that we keep His commandments." And as all His commandments are righteousness; as the keeping of His commandments is the manifestation of the love of God in the life; and as this love of God is shed abroad in the life by the Holy Spirit, this is the righteousness of the law, which is fulfilled in us, who walk not after the flesh but after the Spirit.

Thus, as the Holy Spirit is the seal of righteousness, it is only by means of the Holy Spirit of God that the mark of God can be put upon us in our words, actions, and characters, in our honor of Immanuel. And in truth it is indeed the Holy Spirit of God "by whom you were sealed for the day of redemption." Eph. 4:30. And "the time has come when all who work in Christ's lines will have the mark of God."

Have you the mark of God? Have you the seal of the righteousness of God? If not, why not? When the righteousness of God is a free gift to everybody, why do you not accept it? You never find any difficulty in accepting a free gift that is bestowed by a man: why should you find any difficulty in accepting this free gift bestowed upon you by the Lord?

Accept then, in all its fulness, the righteousness of God which is freely given. Then, upon this, receive the promise of the Spirit through faith. Then still look to that Spirit and depend upon him to impart to you the righteousness of God, to perfect in you the work of Christ and to seal you "for the day of redemption."

And the day of redemption is at the doors. This is certain; for when the man clothed in linen, with the writer's inkhorn by his side, was commanded to "go through the midst of the city, . . . and put a mark on the foreheads of the men who sigh and cry over all the abominations that are done within it," to the others who had the destroying weapons in their hands it was said, "Go after him through thebcity and kill: . . . but do not come near anyone on whom is the mark; and begin at My sanctuary" (Eze. 9:1–6). The ones with the destroying weapons follow shortly, if not closely, "after him" who puts the mark of God. And as "the time has now come when the mark of God" is being set, it can not be long ere the ones with the destroying weapons will pass through also.

Have you the righteousness of God imputed and imparted, which God can seal by his Holy Spirit? It is a free gift to every one who believes.

"Ask, and it will be given to you." "Receive the Holy Spirit." "Be filled with" "the Holy Spirit of God, by whom you were sealed for the day of redemption."

The Advent Review and Sabbath Herald, December 20, 1898, p. 814.

Sealed

"AND do not grieve the Holy Spirit of God, by whom you were sealed for the day of redemption" (Eph. 4:30). When anything is sealed, it is made secure; and God by His Holy Spirit is now sealing hearts for eternity. Will you let the Holy Spirit do His work in you? Let him, let him!

The Advent Review and Sabbath Herald, December 20, 1898, p. 817.

Chapter 24—Baptized By The Spirit

People receive the Spirit of God when they are baptized with the Holy Spirit. They are by Him baptized into divine unity—the unity for which Jesus prayed.

"For by one Spirit we were all baptized into one body—whether Jews or Greeks, whether slaves or free—and have all been made to drink into one Spirit" (1 Cor. 12:13). And this unity is one of both individual and mutual helpfulness and dependence.

It is the unity of individual and mutual helpfulness; because the Holy Spirit is given alone to fit us for service. And so it is written: "The Spirit of the Lord God is upon Me, because the Lord has anointed Me to preach good tidings to the poor; He has sent Me to heal the brokenhearted, to proclaim liberty to the captives, And the opening of the prison to those who are bound" (Isa. 61:1). And, "God anointed Jesus of Nazareth with the Holy Spirit and with power, who went about doing good and healing all who were oppressed by the devil, for God was with Him" (Acts 10:38).

It is also the unity of individual and mutual dependence; because the gifts of the Spirit are many, and are divided "to each one individually as He wills" (1 Cor. 12:11). These gifts are given "for the edifying of the body of Christ," "which is the church." Each gift is essential to the church. But as no one person has all the gifts, each one is dependent upon all the others for the benefits which each gift imparts to the church.

Therefore it is written: "God has set the members, each one of them, in the body just as He pleased. And if they were all one member, where would the body be? But now indeed there are many members, yet one body. And the eye cannot say to the hand, "I have no need of you"; nor again the head to the feet, "I have no need of you." No, much rather, those members of the body which seem to be weaker are necessary. And those members of the body which we think to be less honorable, on these we bestow greater honor; and our unpresentable parts have greater modesty" (1 Cor. 12:18–23).

Just as the human body is composed of many members, and each member in its place is essential to the symmetry of the body; and just as each member of the human body, however small and feeble, or however great and strong, is dependent on every other member of the body, in order to the proper action of the body as God designed it; so is the body of Christ—the church. And as under "the inspiration of the Almighty," there is a divine unity in the human body, so under the baptism of the Holy Spirit, the inspiration of the Almighty, there is divine unity in the body of Christ, which is the church.

Under the reign of the Holy Spirit, no member of the church can say of another, "I have no need of you;" even the head cannot say to the feet, "I have no need of you." How much less, then, can any member of the body say to another member, "I have no need of you." For "God composed the body, having given greater honor to that part which lacks it, that there should be no schism in the body, but that the members should have the same care for one another. And if one member suffers, all the members suffer with it; or if one member is honored, all the members rejoice with it" (1 Cor. 12:24–26).

"Now you are the body of Christ, and members individually" (v. 27). And Christ is now baptizing His people with the Holy Spirit into this divine unity of the church of Christ. Thank the Lord! Are you baptized into this divine unity? or is there division where you are? Is Christ divided?—No, no! "By one Spirit we were all baptized into one body," as certainly as we are baptized with the Spirit at all. Are you baptized with the Holy Spirit?

"Ask, and it will be given to you." "Receive the Holy Spirit." "Be filled with" "the Holy Spirit of God, by whom you were sealed for the day of redemption."

The Advent Review and Sabbath Herald, January 3, 1899.

Chapter 25—The Unity Of The Spirit

While the great object of the gift, and the gifts, of the Holy Spirit is the perfection of the believers, yet this cannot be attained without the unity of the believers.

For it is written of the gifts of the Spirit that they are "for the equipping of the saints . . . till we all come to the unity of the faith and of the knowledge of the Son of God, to a perfect man, to the measure of the stature of the fullness of Christ" (Eph. 4:12, 13).

This unity of the believers is the great longing of Christ, the one great thing for which He prayed. "I do not pray for these alone, but also for those who will believe in Me through their word; that they all may be one;" "that they may be one;" "that they may be made perfect in one." (John 17:20–23).

He also indicates what is the character of this unity: "As You, Father, are in Me, and I in You, that they also may be one in Us;" "that they may be one, just as We are one: I in them, and You in Me, that they may be made perfect in one." This unity of the believers is the divine unity itself; for it is just "as" is the unity between the divine Father and the divine Son.

But without the divine nature, how can divine unity ever be found among men? As they are naturally, men have not the Spirit of unity, but the spirit of enmity. "The carnal mind is enmity against God." And being enmity against God, it results in putting men at enmity with one another. And so men always and everywhere have drawn lines, and built up walls of separation between themselves,—national lines, tribal lines, aristocratic lines, society lines, color lines, sectarian lines, etc., etc., etc.

But Jesus Christ "is our peace, who has made both one, and has broken down the middle wall of separation, having abolished in His flesh the enmity, . . . so as to create in Himself one new man from the two, thus making peace, and that He might reconcile them both to God in one body through the cross, thereby putting to death the enmity. And He came and preached peace to you who were afar off and to those who were near. For through Him we both have access by one Spirit to the Father" (Eph. 2:13-18).

The cross of Christ destroys the enmity against God, and also breaks down all the lines of separation and walls of partition which, by the working of this enmity, men have made between themselves; and the "one Spirit" takes all these in whom the enmity has been destroyed by beholding the cross of Christ, and binds them all in "one body" in divine unity.

So unless men are partakers of the divine nature, they can never enter into this divine unity which is the characteristic of the church of Christ, and for which the Lord so earnestly prayed; and without the Holy Spirit of God, men cannot be partakers of the divine nature. For God being Spirit, and the Holy Spirit being the Spirit of God, He is of the divine nature; and whoever is partaker of the Holy Spirit, is thereby partaker of the divine nature.

Thus it is alone the baptism of the Holy Spirit that can bring the disciples of Christ into that unity for which He prayed: "that they all may be one, as You, Father, are in Me, and I in You; that they also may be one in Us" (John 17:21). Therefore it is written: "I will pray the Father, and He will give you another Helper, that He may abide with you forever—the Spirit of truth. . . . I will not leave you orphans; I will come to you. . . . At that day you will know that I am in My Father, and you in Me, and I in you" (John 14:16–20).

He who is partaker of the Holy Spirit, he who is baptized with the Holy Spirit, by that very fact is made acquainted with the divine unity of the Father and the Son; and is himself bound into that divine unity. And this unity of the Spirit with the Father and the Son is so precious that he would rather die than to be separated from it. And all who know this unity of the Spirit are one, wherever or whoever they may be: they are one as the Father and the Son are one; because their fellowship of the Spirit is the fellowship of the Father and the Son. By one Spirit are they all baptized into one body; and that body is the body of Christ, in whom God—yes, all the fullness of the Godhead bodily—dwells.

This is the unity of the true believers in Jesus. Not the unity that ought to be; no, this is the unity that there is everywhere among the true believers in Jesus. It is divine unity. It is the unity of the Spirit, in the Spirit, with the Father and the Son.

"Ask, and it will be given to you." "Receive the Holy Spirit." "Be filled with" "the Holy Spirit of God, by whom you were sealed for the day of redemption."

The Advent Review and Sabbath Herald, January 17, 1899.

Chapter 26—The Spirit Teaches Us

Of the Holy Spirit, Jesus said, "He will glorify Me, for He will take of what is Mine and declare it to you" (John 16:14).

To declare a thing is to call special attention to it, to point out its attractions and its value.

This is what the Holy Spirit does to us with the things of God. He takes the things of God, and presents them to our view, makes them plain to our understanding.

This must needs be, because these great things are so far beyond our view and our comprehension that "eye has not seen, nor ear heard, nor have entered into the heart of man the things which God has prepared for those who love Him" (1 Cor. 2:9).

But in His mercy and His gentleness, the Lord gives all these things into the charge of the Spirit, to "declare" to us; "for the Spirit searches all things, yes, the deep things of God" (1 Cor. 2:10).

Nor is it only that He "searches all things," but He is to declare to us "all things;" for Jesus said, "All things that the Father has are Mine. Therefore I said that He will take of Mine and declare it to you" (John 16:15).

All the wealth, all the glory, all the beauty, of all the wonderful things of God are free to us; nothing is kept back. That we might know all these things, is one reason that the Holy Spirit is given. These things are of eternal depth and infinite compass, and only "the eternal Spirit" can fully fathom them. "Even so no one knows the things of God except the Spirit of God" (1 Cor. 2:11). Therefore it is He to whom it is given to declare them to us.

"But the Helper, the Holy Spirit, whom the Father will send in My name, He will teach you all things, and bring to your remembrance all things that I said to you" (John 14:26).

What a wonderful Teacher! What a wonderful school! A university, yes, the university, indeed. Have you entered the school? Have you this wonderful Teacher?

"Ask, and it will be given to you." "Receive the Holy Spirit." "For everyone who asks receives." "Be filled with" "the Holy Spirit of God, by whom you were sealed for the day of redemption."

For more than a year, in the demonstration and power of the Spirit, the message has been going to this people, "Receive the Holy Spirit." And what is His office?—"And do not grieve the Holy Spirit of God, by whom you were sealed for the day of redemption." The day of redemption is right at hand. Would you be sealed? Then now, just now, surrender to the instrumentality that will accomplish this result.

The Advent Review and Sabbath Herald, February 28, 1899.

Other books by Ellen G. White that have not been previously published:

1. 1888 Materials Volume 1.
2. 1888 Materials Volume 2.
3. 1888 Materials Volume 3.
4. 1888 Materials Volume 4.
5. Lessons from the Life of Solomon.
6. Exhaustive Commentary on Genesis.
7. Exhaustive Commentary on Daniel.
8. Exhaustive Commentary on Revelation.
9. The Life of Paul: Lessons.
10. Healthful Living
11. Christian Temperance and Biblical Hygiene.
12. 1888 Sermons.
13. Spalding and Magan Collection.
14. Letters to Battle Creek.
15. Loma Linda messages.
16. The Young Instructor Volume 1 (Original Articles).
17. The Young Instructor Volume 2 (Original Articles).

¡¡¡¡¡¡¡MORE WILL BE AVAILABLE!!!!!!

*If you want to buy them in bulk (40% discount), they are in boxes of 50 books (can be mixed) and you can contact us at this email:
lsdistribution07@gmail.com

Other 1888 Message books available:

1. Discovering the Cross, Author: Robert J. Wieland.
2. Introduction to the Message of 1888, Author: Robert J. Wieland.
3. 1888 Reexamined, Authors: Robert J. Wieland and Donald K. Short.
4. Behold, I stand at the Door and knock, Author: Robert J. Wieland.
5. Ten Great Truths of the Gospel, Author: Robert J. Wieland.
6. Our Glorious Future, Author: Robert J. Wieland.
7. Modern Revivals, Author: Robert J. Wieland.
8. The Word Became Flesh, Author: Ralph Larson.
9. Christology in the Writings of Ellen G. White, Author: Ralph Larson.
10. The Gospel in Galatians, Author: E. J. Waggoner.
11. Letter to the Romans, Author: E. J. Waggoner.
12. The Everlasting Covenant, Author: E. J. Waggoner.
13. Christ and His Righteousness, Author: E. J. Waggoner.
14. 1888 Materials; Volumes 1-4 in Spanish, Author: Ellen G. White.
15. The Consecrated Path to Christian Perfection, Author: A. T. Jones.
16. The Third Angel's Message; 3 Volumes, Author: A. T. Jones.
17. Lessons on Faith, Authors: A. T. Jones and E. J. Waggoner.
18. The Man of Romans 7: Ralph Larson & Ellet J. Waggoner.

¡¡¡¡¡¡¡AND MORE WILL COME!!!!!!

*If you wish to purchase them in bulk (40% discount), they are by boxes of 50 books (can be mixed) and you can contact us at this email:
lsdistribution07@gmail.com